Shambles to Stained Glass

Chloe Hasden

BookLeaf
Publishing

India | USA | UK

Presentation by *BookLeaf Publishing*

Web: www.bookleafpub.com

E-mail: info@bookleafpub.com

ISBN:9789358315493

First edition 2024

to emmett, who makes everything brighter

Table of Contents

d i s g r a c e

You told me not to cry,
but a tear fell down my face.

disgrace

You told me to hold my shoulders back,
but I could not bear the weight.

disgrace

You told me to act like a lady,
but I slipped in my high heels.

disgrace

You told me that I'd be okay,
and I believed that time could heal.

Pieces

You broke me to pieces,
you left me as glass.
You watched as I stepped on
my own shards
and you just laughed.

You left me in pieces,
you left me as glass.

But you best believe that
I am stronger now,
I'm better
and I'm back.

You left me in pieces.

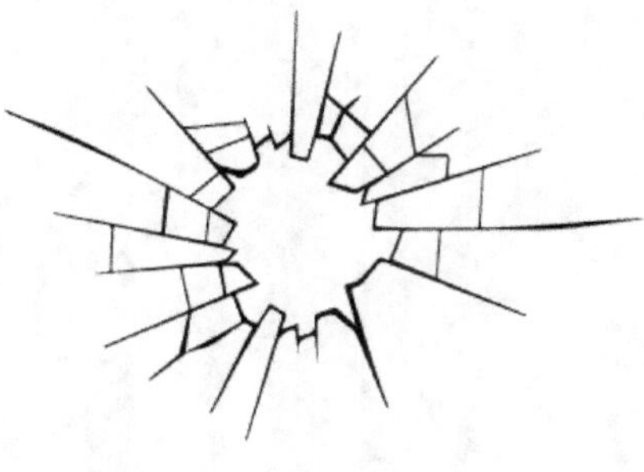

Desert Love

Dust covers the sunlight
and I begged for the rain,
but the dust didn't stop
the heat of the day.
I've never wished my days away
but I wish for the sun to go down,
'cause the moonlight means freedom
and I wish from death
as I stare into the limited that is limitless.

Cloud Nine Haze

And maybe if you had told me,
I could've understood you more clearly.
'Cause my head's been up in the clouds these
days,
but it ain't cloud nine that I'm feeling.

When you're in a daze for a million days,
all the vitamin D it just turns to haze.
And I hate to tell ya, but my car's been broke.
I can't count on my high beams to get me
through.

You've convinced me that different humans
awaken different beasts in everyone.
I've befriended them, no losing them -
my demons know how to swim.

No sinking, only taming,
guarding and playing.
'Cause I rise high, I fall hard,
I hit a rock bottom pitfall.

I see embers crashing
to the ground.
Fire still smoking,
not going out.

Strong woman, weak universe.
Short leashes on giant teeth.
I see no mercy, only hurting.
Daze for days on end.

The dodging and kicking,
It's gotta come to an end.
And I gotta find it from deep within.
before it's killing me slowly from the outside
in.

I need my car checked,
get my brights back on.
And maybe, you could tell me
so I can get on cloud nine.

untitled

You don't know what you've got 'til it's gone,
or maybe you just thought you'd never lose it.
The truth is we forget we're mortal and that
we cannot stop the time;
that we are not invincible and things can slip
away.
Out of reach, out of touch, out of order,
try again at a later time.
But until then, tell me you love me
while I'm here to sound a reply.

i sat down to write you

i sat down to write you
a sad little song
that came from a soul
rooted in dust

melancholy, i called it
but i dug my fingertips
as deep as i could
into myself

and as i wrote,
bits of pencil chipped away
tormented years of
my own shadowed heart

slowly and surely
i could see what once was there
was there all along
climbing back to the surface

the tune changed
a sad little song
turned to a
triumphant symphony

run toward what
sets you on fire
and don't apologize
for running

fall into the discovery
of the flowers
that bloom in the
sunlight and the shade

do the best you can
and that is enough
you are enough
you are worthy

you've never been right
here in this moment before
we're all brand new
we're all in this together

you can find a safe place
if you need a break
or you can burst through
if you can't contain your joy

the sunlight that
covers the earth
has enough sunshine
for every one of us

and what a beautiful,
beautiful thing it is
to simply live
as yourself, whole

i sat down to write you
a sad little song
but now i find myself
singing

Blooming

Fighting with time, fighting with them
Fighting things from deep within
And I know the world is spinning
But I'm just standing still

I am patient with people
but impatient with time
I find myself simply waiting,
waiting to bloom

As if I haven't been blooming all along

The Home I Built

I myself am a home
built with grit and grace and time.
I am boards of bravery,
together with nails divine.

I am the words I've written
and I am the songs I sing,
the flowers that I've planted
and the tender-heartedness I bring.

I am the summer heat in August
and rain showers come the spring,
I am wonder in the darkness
and the hope in shiny things.

Breathe into me,
Breathe out.
I am just what I speak.

we can

can you believe we are in a world
with autumns that bring us mums and
leaves of warmer colors

and we are in a world
with paw prints in the sand and
chirps of birds around us

can you believe we are in a world
that offers both shade and sunshine
when we need it

and we are in a world
where we can choose to be and believe
and we can choose to create and wonder

can you believe we live in a world
that gives us people with shoulders
to lean on and ears to listen

and in the hard it gives us
grace and lessons and trials and
when it feels just like we can't

can you believe we live in a world
where we can

Only Pack the Essentials

The weight was heavy -
I watched outside of myself as threads
unraveled.
The handle couldn't even
bear the weight

I carried it all
the weight of the world
the worries and fears and needs
of other people -
what's theirs is mine

The weight was heavy -
I watched outside of myself as the load
drooped and
my shoulders fell
with it, but soon

I left behind a pile of regrets,
the instances of doubt
confusion
The tasks that were not
even mine to complete

But what I took was far more liberating,
wonder and promise and grace
the chances I took,
the patience I held
and all the love

And then, I took a breath.

Motherhood Unfolding

Before my hands even held you,
I embraced your presence-
your little lovetaps to my insides
like the slightest breeze
in the August heat.

Once our hands touched,
and our chests bare and beating together,
my heart found its home
where every smile, laugh, move I make
starts with you.

Becoming your mother changed me...
I am different than I once was.
Out of me, you made a protector,
A whimsical force to be reckoned with.
My once dainty and fragile feathers turned to
stark and heavy wings.

With truth, grace, and promise
I tell you that I will love you forever.
No ruse, no conditions, no fingers crossed.
My heart needed you-
And for you, I will always be home.

I Wonder About the Stars

I wonder about the stars
and if they know
how they shine

Or if the sun
ever smiles knowing
how it warms us

Does the moon
ever chuckle as it
lights up the night sky

I wonder about my neighbor
and if they know how I watch
over their house when they're gone

Or if the dogs I smile at
on the street know
that they bring me joy

Does the church ever close
its doors to many full pews
and sigh a sigh of gratitude

I wonder about the ways
that I wonder about all
the little things in life

And the ways in which
I celebrate others
for simply existing

Do I ever close my eyes
and think to myself
'you, my dear, are deserving'

How I Love that Girl

20 years ago, I met a girl
who created without containment.
She was her own, she stood her ground,
she laughed till she couldn't stand it.

15 years ago, we crossed paths once more,
she smiled a bit more timidly.
But I saw the glimmer in her eyes -
the ones that saw life so vividly.

10 years ago, she'd grown so much
and felt everything so deep.
She dreamt big dreams for herself
and I watched her take a leap.

5 years ago, she wondered
if she'd ever make it through,
but felt a hand scoop her up
the way that angels do.

I spoke to her just yesterday
and then I watched her smile.
Oh, how I love that girl who
loves with the heart of a child.

Don't Mind Me

Don't mind me,
I'm just figuring it out.
I've done a lot
but there's so much left.

Don't mind me,
I'm just playing bumper cars.
There's really no direction,
is there?

Don't mind me,
I'm just falling from the trees.
Floating down the blue, blue sky
making peace with my landing.

Don't mind me,
I'm just jumping from my nest.
Watch me -
I'm flying

Me for Me

My life changed when I took a chance on
myself.

evergreen

I caught myself spinning a lazy susan
on the soft pine table
with dents and scribbles from childhood and
teeth marks on the edge,
no doubt from
the toothy grins of littles
when they needed comfort

'I am pine,' I thought in the moment
I can be anything
I am rooted in love
I can survive
Earth Wind Water
But, too
I am soft
I believe in a future
so bright and a linkage
to renewal

I am

evergreen

Hauntingly Beautiful

There is power in the strokes of a pen and a
paintbrush and they speak without saying
anything at all.
There is grace in the hug or the smile from a
stranger who is tethered to this life just like
you and doing their best just like you.
There is hope from the words of mouths that
don't speak like you and none of it is the
same, but it is, isn't it?
The way we were all given a chance to make
the most of the mountains we've been placed
on
and the way we can hold hands to help each
other across bridges and to soar across the
sky
and how liberating it is to know that we can
connect
no matter what.
And together, we can heal

ourselves

and

each other.

Corridor

I live in a corridor.
Measured distances between the doors,
but there is anything but symmetry.

Take me to the low-down locked doors,
secrets with shattered glass;
the sum of diabolical heartbreak
and totem poles of confused, lost souls
stranded and grasping at torn shreds
of hope for another life.
Take me to the crystal knobs
electrified with passion
and blown-up dreams of solitude
and celestial smiles;
riding on the backs of the powerful
strong with heart and will.

Take me to the cracked panels where the light
shines through -
seeping with survival,
but coated with delectable spirits
marveling on what is and
hoping for what's to come.

Take me to the room of wonder -
seductive desires, pulsating beings;
chances and far pleasures
justified with love and fervor -
A hearty glow of strength
from the most beloved tenderness.

I live in a corridor.
Measured distances between the doors,
but there is anything but symmetry.

This is for you

This is for all the ones who stood up for
something and someone and themselves
even when it was hard and grueling and the
lump in your throat was ever growing;
when you thought you had no fight left but
something kept telling you to push.
This is for all the ones who did for others
what they wouldn't do for themselves
and the ones who covered others in praise to
hide their own pain and
it's also for the ones who decided not to blink
back the tears any longer
because if rain can grow the flowers,
then it can't hurt you.
This is for all the ones whose hearts spoke
through tears and who knew all the words yet
had nothing to say.
This is for all the ones who grew in ways
they'd never imagined possible and thanked
others before themselves.

I see you.

This is for you.

Beloved

A sacred voice calls me beloved
I shutter - I am so unworthy.
His hand is on me every time.
I tremble - through my hard, He shows me
grace.
My heart swells
I am pushed against the sides,
but I only grow
in love.
I brace myself for the burst,
but I am only stretched by the spirit.
Overflowing with love
I shutter - it is unbridled joy.
I am derailed, but I'm still held.
I tremble - a sacred voice calls me beloved.

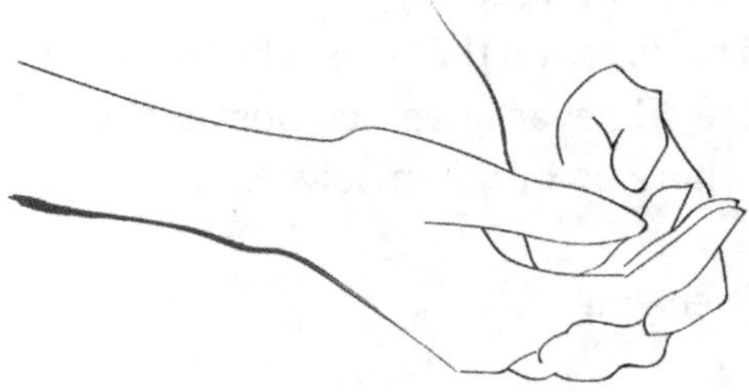

Stained Glass Girl

She sparkled when the light hit,
That girl.

She filled her cracks with gold
and glitter
and when the light went out
you could still see
the red in her cheeks
from laughter
and the way her blue eyes
reminded you of the sea at dusk
and when she loved
you felt the gold thicken
together and
you just knew that she
had a soul that dreamed
a thousand dreams
that she couldn't
yet put words to
and her yellow hair,
like sunshine,
bounced in her ponytail
joyfully
and you smiled to yourself
as you watched her learn

to walk hand in hand with herself
and you smiled again because what she didn't
know, but what you had always known -

is that she shone from within,
That girl.